MEOWS AND PURRS

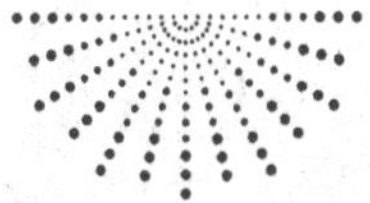

DEBBIE DE LOUISE

This collection of poems is dedicated in honor of my three cats, Stripey, Harry, and Hermione and to the memories of all the cats before them. It's also dedicated to my mother who taught me how to love and care for animals.

Some of these poems are funny; others are sad, but they all reflect the special nature of cats. Cat lovers will recognize the different personalities and traits that they are familiar with and enjoy in their own cats.

MY MOTHER'S CATS

My earliest memories
were of my mother's cats
the lost and the strays
those she fed outside
those she kept
those she gave away.

There were always cats in our house, it seems
tabbies, shorthairs, Siamese

We had litters of kittens
a few older cats
some were thin
others fat.

A few lived with us long
a few very short
they were each special
I thought.

My mother's cats
were my friends

a young child, almost an only
they kept me company.

My mother's cats
knew when I was sad or sick
They comforted me with purrs and licks

My mother taught me
how to care for them
the special bond of a furry friend

We cried together
when they died
buried them in our backyard

My love of cats was born in childhood
raised over years
by a woman so good

Now that she's gone
I know what she left me
a heart full of love for all felines
along with the memories.

*This poem is dedicated to Florence Smiloff, my cat
loving mother, who passed away in 2018.

KITTY, LITTLE GIRL, AND PUMPKIN

The summer I was five,
my mother and I
found a lost cat in the park.
She was gray with a white streak down her
    nose.
We took her home.

In October,
Kitty gave birth in my closet.
I named one of the kittens Pumpkin
even though he was gray.
Two years later, he disappeared with his
    brother.
Kitty and her daughter, Little Girl, lived to
    old age.

The summer I was twenty-five,
Kitty died.
I buried her in my garden
under the marigolds.
A year later, Little Girl joined her mother.

I've had many cats since then,
but I still remember Kitty, Little Girl, and
    Pumpkin.

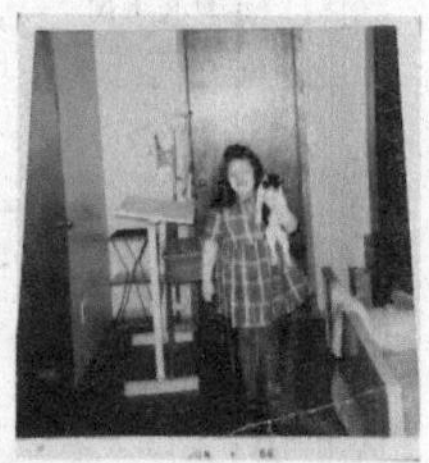

MY BENNY BOY

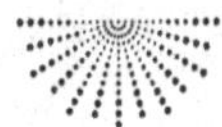

Benny was my boy.
He loved to jump high
and watch birds fly.

He was a gray, shorthaired cat.
The sweetest boy I ever had.

Benny didn't live long.
He suffered kidney disease young.
Mom and I tried fluid therapy and prayer.
It was a losing battle, we feared.

I remember the day that fall
I rushed home after Mom's call.
She was crying
Benny was dying

He sat on my lap in the car
silently purring as I stroked his head
He raised it weakly
He was nearly dead.

The vet put him to rest
I knew it was for the best
but I missed him so
I've never forgotten my Benny boy.

FLOPPY

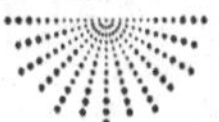

I had a cat named Floppy
back in the nineteen nineties.
He was named for floppy disks
but was gray and white like a bunny.
I found him in a department store's pet
    section
with his three brothers.

I was just married and took him home to my
    apartment.
He was a tiny kitten.
I soon found out he had asthma
and had to take medicine.

He joined us after Halloween
and found a lollipop in a basket.
After that, he made a game
of kicking them under our refrigerator.

A few years later,
he got diabetes.
I injected him with insulin

twice a day.
He also got liver issues
and pancreatitis.

He was hospitalized three times.
The last time, I had to say goodbye.
He was fifteen
when that happened,
and I was heartbroken.
It was like losing a child, a baby.
I'll always remember my Floppy.

*Floppy was a special cat of mine. He was the first cat
I had after I married.

FERAL

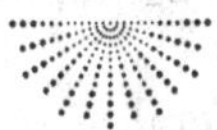

She was feral
born outside and abandoned
An orange cat with pretty green eyes.
She wasn't very old and a bit rare.
Most red tabbies are males,
I hear.

I took her home
and named her Holly.
She cried for several days
and tried to escape.

We had another cat.
He helped her adjust.
He taught her how to use the litter pan
and live inside.

Holly liked to play
with toy mice.
She ran after them down the hall.
She wasn't with us long.
She grew a sarcoma on her back.

We had to remove it,
but the cancer returned.
We had to let her go.

I used up boxes of tissues with my tears.
A year later, my daughter was born.
I named her Holly
after my beloved feral.

*My mother was caring for Holly outside in her back-
yard and asked me if I wanted to take her. Floppy was
three years old at the time, and I was worried that
they wouldn't get along. As it turned out, he took her
under his wing and even taught her how to use the
litter box. She died a few years before him, but she
was more attached to him than he was to her. When
he was away at the animal hospital, the three times he
was treated for his various illnesses, she missed him
very much and was happy when he came home.

ODE TO OLIVER

There's a spot next to my pillow that's bare.
Oliver always used to sleep there.
He loved me to stroke his chest.
Of all my cats, he was one of the best.

He was a handsome Siamese cat.
There was no doubt about that.
Although we only had him four years,
I can't help shedding so many tears.

His favorite spot was his cat bed.
It's so hard to believe he's dead.
He did such cute things in the past,
like fishing in his water bowl where he made
    quite a splash.

He loved to be brushed,
and his fur was so lush.
His loud voice in the morning was my alarm
    clock.
Losing him is still a shock.

But he's out of pain now on Rainbow Bridge
    waiting for me
with my other special cats who one day
    I'll see.

*Oliver was my mother's cat. She was very attached to him. When Hurricane Sandy hit and she was without electricity, she refused to leave her home unless Oliver came with her. We took them both until she had her power back. A few years later, we adopted Oliver after my mother went into a nursing home. He was a senior cat of twelve when he joined our family, and we had him for five wonderful years. My daughter and I fell in love with him. He was a sweet boy who was friendly and affectionate to everyone. He died nine months before my mother. Because of her dementia, we never told her.

OVER THE RAINBOW BRIDGE

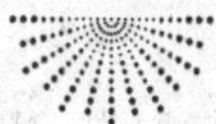

They scamper about
healthy, happy
tails held high
no more pain
young again.

Coats are shiny
eyes are bright.
They only miss
their human's sight.

Gathering above the clouds
they look down
hoping for a glance
a memory, a touch
They hated to leave
but had no choice.
They had to go
over the Rainbow Bridge.

RIGHT CAT AT THE WRONG TIME

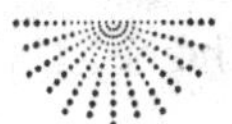

He was given to us
after we lost our boy
to mend our hearts
and bring some joy.

It didn't turn out the way
we expected.
I got sick, couldn't breathe.
The doctors thought
I was infected.

I spent a week in the hospital.
The final diagnosis was that I had asthma,
couldn't keep a cat.

I'd had cats all my life
without a problem.
They told me it happens.
They were sorry.

I found a temporary home
for my new kitten, Stripey

until I was better
and could care for him.

Because of that
we didn't bond or get close
It was hard for the cat,
but it wasn't my choice.

It took some time
before Stripey could come into my room
or sleep on my bed.
He got attached to my husband instead.

I didn't mind
but still felt bad.
It wasn't his fault or mine
that he was the right cat at the wrong time.

Stripey is currently 13 years old.
He's seen another come and go.
He now lives with two others
a sister and a brother.
I'm so glad they're together.
I love them all so.

*Our neighbor was trying to find a home for a stray tabby cat after we lost Floppy. We'd been felineless for a year and wasn't sure if we were ready for another cat. However, we adopted him on our anniversary, and the rest of his story is in this poem. When we took Oliver from my mother, it wasn't an easy adjustment, but they settled in together. About a year after Oliver died, we adopted our current cats, Harry and Hermione, who were then three-month old kittens. It also took time for Stripey to accept the new additions, but now they all hang out together. Stripey currently suffers from hyperthyroidism but is doing well on daily medication. Harry and Hermione have grown into beautiful three-year-old cats.

CAT CAFÉ

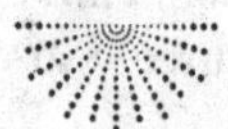

Room full of cats
Room full of people
Black kitten by the window
Silky fur, big golden eyes
playful yet a little shy
Waiting for us
Can we take him home?
He's part of a pair
Sweet calico
pretty tri-colored girl
tail held high without fear
Waiting for us
Can we take two?
Room in our home
Room in our lives
We lost our senior boy last year

*This poem was based on our adoption of Harry and
Hermione after Oliver died. We adopted them from
the Shabby Tabby Cat Café on Long Island, but they

came from the Golden Paws Society Rescue in Huntington. While we still had Stripey, my daughter wanted a cat to replace Oliver. She'd always wanted a black cat, so when she saw Harry, she fell in love. We didn't realize that he had a sister, a dilute calico named Hermione, but when we were told they had to be adopted together, we were somewhat hesitant. I've never regretted taking them both. My daughter considers herself their mother, and I'm their grandmother. We love them dearly.

MINI PANTHER

Mini Panther
Dark as night
Golden eyes shining bright.

Tame yet wild
Stalking prey
On a string I wave.

Crouching low
Ready to spring
At the sound
Of the catfood tin.

Mini Panther
Sleek and slim
Sturdy body, long lean limbs

Tiny black kitten
Now full grown
My Mini Panther guards our home.

*This poem is dedicated to Harry, my handsome and friendly mini panther.

I KNOW A CALICO

I know a calico
who crosses her paws
kneads soft blankets,
pillows, and throws.

I know a calico
with pretty green eyes
a tri-color tail
and the sweetest cry.

I know a calico
who plays with toy coils
bats them under chairs
and around the floor.

I know a calico
who purrs when you pet her
perches in high places
tops of closets and refrigerators.

I know a calico
Who's smart and wise

when you take her photo,
she closes her eyes.

I know a calico
who growls at strangers by the door
chatters when she hears birds call.

I know a calico
with white boots and gloves
a precious cat anyone would love.

I know a calico who deserves a poem
She's the one who lives in my home.

*This poem is dedicated to my beautiful and sweet
cat, Hermione.

MY FURRY MUSES

They sit by my keyboard
when I write,
block the screen from my sight.

I don't find it amusing,
this habit of my furry muses.

I love to include cats in my books and stories.
They're great at finding clues and solving
    mysteries.

They're funny and wise.
People like to read about their antics,
the crazy things they do often surprise.

My furry muses are special to me.
I never suffer from writer's block.
They help me recognize when ideas knock.

They steal my pens
and chew on my charging wires,

but I'd have it no other way.
My furry muses always inspire,
and so they stay.

TWO CATS ARE BETTER THAN ONE

Double the trouble,
double the fun.
Two cats are better than one.

When you look to adopt a kitten,
ask for a sibling or two.
It's the best thing you can do.

You'll never regret taking another.
They'll grow up as friends and play together.

Don't worry about the litter pans.
They'll share one box of sand.

No cat food will go to waste.
Just pick up a case.

Make room on your bed and under the covers.
You'll never be lonely with one or the other.

Double the charm,

double the love.
Two cats are better than one.

If you open your heart to two fur babies,
You'll know it's the best things you've done
because two cats are better than one.

CATS BY DAY AND NIGHT

Harry in the morning
black head resting against my pillow
his purrs wake me softly
I run my hands through his silky fur
the day brightens

I dress and shower
say goodbye to my cats
hard to leave for work
seeing sad furry faces
I'll be back.

I visit for lunch
serve their favorite treats
All three gather round to snack
Stripey rubs my ankles with his cheeks
the day brightens

I close the door
wave to my cats in the windows
watching me go
sad furry faces

I'll be back.

I arrive home
greeted by all three
I feed them before I eat
I'm glad to be back
with my fur babies

Hermione at night
white paws on my sheets
kneading a gentle lullaby
I fall asleep to the rhythm of her strokes
the night brightens

THE CHRISTMAS MITTEN

Three years ago at Christmas
I got my kitten a mitten.
I put it in her stocking.
When I gave it to her,
she hid it.

I looked all over
for her hiding spot.
I couldn't find it anywhere
until she pulled it out
from under a chair.

My kitten, now a cat
still has that mitten.
It's raggedy and worn
but she doesn't care about that.

She carries it in her mouth
like a mother carries her kitten.
I find it in the oddest places
that old Christmas mitten.

*My Hermione still has this raggedy mitten after three years.

BOXES AND BAGS

Don't buy cat toys with expensive tags.
Your cats only need
boxes and bags.

They'll crawl inside
a cardboard hideaway
and camouflage themselves
from invisible prey.

If you have two cats or more,
They'll be occupied
taking turns jumping inside.

It could get noisy
with crinkling and drags.
Cats just love their boxes and bags.

They rip them up,
make them a house.
It's almost as fun
as catching a mouse.

So save your packages
and make your cats happy
with simple pleasures.
Boxes and bags are their fondest treasures.

CAT (HAIKU)

Playful purring pet
Furry funny feline friend.
Cuddly, crazy, cat!

CAT DOOR

In and out
Out and in
Cats like to go
wherever they can.

When they see a closed door,
their scratching and crying,
you can't ignore.

Up and down
Down and up
Answer their pleas.
They won't stop.

In and out
Out and in
Cats like to go
Whenever they can.

Buy a cat flap or door
And let your cats explore.

You'll get some rest
And much more peace.
The only way their demands will cease.

In and out
Out and in
Through the cat door
Again and again.

ACROBATS AND CLOWNS

Anyone who's lived with cats
knows what they're about.
They climb and jump like acrobats.
They make you smile when you're down,
funny, furry, feline clowns.

The things they do you question why.
They can soar through the air
in pursuit of a fly.
They can squeeze
into the smallest places
and make the funniest faces.

When something catches their eye,
their whiskers twitch
and strange sounds they emit.

They're daredevils
and yoga masters,
thieves and actors
but most of their renown
are as acrobats and clowns.

THE ZOOMIES

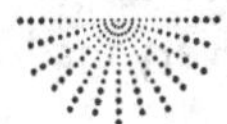

A flash of fur
So fast it's a blur.

Early morning and at dusk
they race around the house.
Pent-up energy flows free
during The Zoomies.

It's a sight to see and hear.
One minute they're down the hall;
the next they're everywhere.

There's disarray in their wake.
Papers scattered, chairs overturned,
but it's only play, I've learned.

When The Zoomies hit,
they have no choice
but to run all over the place.
It's funny and wild
their feline race.

The Zoomies are a strange phenomenon.
Cat owners can relate
Even the old and quiet ones participate.

After The Zoomies end,
our furry friends crash.
They sleep after every mad dash.

If you hear what sounds like horses' hooves
and feel a strong breeze,
it's not a stampede;
It's The Zoomies.

CAT FIGHT

Claws unsheathed
ear-piercing yowls
bared teeth.
Felines face off in the night
preparing for a cat fight.

Don't interfere
or you'll be slashed
end up with a large gash.
Separate them, make them run.
Your best weapon
a water gun.

Wild beasts
fighting over their domain.
A territory they seek to claim.
A female cat in heat
The Tom's won't retreat.

They'll hiss and bite,
make their mark.

The victor earns the prize
from their cat fight.

LOST CAT

He's back
my lost cat.
After a week of worry
He's returned to me.

I don't know how far he went
in someone's garage or under a fence.

I put up signs
all over the place
offered a reward
if there was any trace.

I prayed each night
that he was safe
and didn't come to a bad fate.

I sent an ad to the papers
called his vet,
but no luck did I get.
Then one morning,
he turned up on my step.

I was so happy
to have him back
my lost cat.

SLEEPING CAT

Tail wrapped around his feet
he sleeps
ears alert
body inert.

His whiskers twitch
when he dreams.
His body shakes
as he wakes.

All afternoon he spends in bed
curled into a furry ball
but at day's end
and in the morn,
he's wide awake
ready to play.

A sleeping cat
prefers your bed
to any pet bed you can buy.
He likes to be near you to lie –

nice, warm, and safe.
It's his most comfortable place.

THE MAGIC OF PURRS

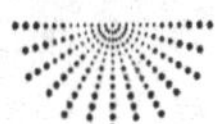

It starts as a rumble
deep in their throat,
then grows loud like a hum.

Cats big and small
make this sound.
It's common to them all.

When they're hungry,
when they're in pain.
a purr is their refrain.

Purring can relax
people as well as cats.

If you want to ease your stress,
don't take a pill.
Pet your cat instead.

The purrs will calm you
and help you bond.
Magic without a wand.

KNEADING

She sits on my bed
paws outstretched.
Claws gently tug
my bedspread.

Along with this action,
she purrs very loud.
Seeing my reaction,
she looks at me proud.

As she squeezes the cloth,
I pet her head.
I'm glad she's careful
not to pull a thread.

Her fingers move to and fro
my little baker kneading dough.

Green eyes half-closed and dreamy.
I snuggle next to her
Soon we'll both be sleeping.

TOE BEANS

I have three cats
with the cutest paws you can see,
they have black, brown, and pink toe beans.

Toe beans are pads
under the toes
These silky skin rounds
cushion the claws.

Most cats have five
like human fingers
Polydactyls have six
It's an extra digit.

Toe beans protect
a kitty's step.
They're squishy and soft
like jelly beans.

A TALE OF TAILS

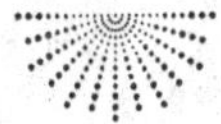

It swishes back and forth
Stands up straight when he's happy
Grows fat in anger
Flat in shame

A tale of tails
is a twisted story behind every cat.
Never close it in the door
Or yank it
You'll regret that.

A tail helps balance
a feline's frame
unless he's a manx
it's as important as his name.

A tale of tails
Can be short or long
Striped or plain
Bushy or tame.

DEBBIE DE LOUISE

A tale of tails
ends at a point
covers the rear
the last thing you see
when a cat disappears

LOAFING

Paws tucked underneath
resembling a loaf of bread.
Kitties may rest in this position
on a chair, couch, or bed.

If you catch your cat loafing,
let him be.
He's very comfy.

You can't tell what they think
when they meditate like a sphynx.

Don't be surprised
if your cat spends hours at a time
sitting this way after his play.

He may not respond
to your call or the sound of the phone.
When he's loafing,
He's in the zone.

The next time you spot

your cat or another feline
looking content and sublime,
gazing rapt
with paws wrapped
posing like a yoga lotus,
let them enjoy their moment of peace.

CAT LADY

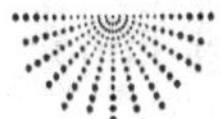

She's a feline fancier
collects cats and cat things,
knicknacks and souvenirs
jewelry and clothing.

The first things she spots
in any store or online
are cat items for sale
and all things feline.

She drinks from cat glasses
uses cat silverware
has a library of cat books
that she stores everywhere.

She drives a car
with a cat license plate
travels to places where cats are well known
and stays at cat inns
but misses her cats at home

She plants catnip in her garden

walks her cats on leashes or in strollers
Her bed and clothes are full of fur
the dander is all over her

A cat sleeps on her pillow
a few by her feet
she won't change position
until they retreat

She decorates with cat trees
and ledges on windows
She even built a catio in her patio

She's very selective
about men who she dates
Here's the trick,
they have to like cats and not be allergic

If you pass by her house
you'll have plenty to see.
A cat wreath graces the door
a welcome mat features paws
Whiskered faces will greet you
all shades and all breeds
from kittens to seniors
so many mouths she feeds

At holiday time
she celebrates with gifts
and stockings for each cat
She's a cat lady
There's no doubt about that.

CAT PHOTOS

You see them every day
all over the Internet.
Facebook, Twitter, Instagram
You name it.

People post photos
of their cats to see
shorthairs, long hairs,
persians, tabbies, Siamese.

If you like looking at cats,
Check out these sites.
A huge number of cat photos
are added each day.
Cats sitting and standing, and at play
even sleeping the day away.

If you think your cat
is model material,
there's a way to find out.
Post her photos online,
see if they go viral after some time.

Dear reader,

We hope you enjoyed reading *Meows And Purrs*. Please take a moment to leave a review, even if it's a short one. Your opinion is important to us.

Discover more books by Debbie De Louise at https://www.nextchapter.pub/authors/debbie-de-louise

Want to know when one of our books is free or discounted? Join the newsletter at http://eepurl.com/bqqB3H

Best regards,

Debbie De Louise and the Next Chapter Team

ACKNOWLEDGMENTS

I'd like to thank the fine staff at Next Chapter especially Miika Hannila who continues to find new ways to market and promote books worldwide. I'm thrilled that my Next Chapter books are available in a wide variety of formats including paperback, eBook, large print, audio, and hardcover with some translated into other languages, as well. I'd also like to acknowledge my fellow Next Chapter authors. I'm honored to be part of this team of talented writers.

Thanks also to my other author friends, my family, and all those who have supported my writing especially my readers who make all the hard work worthwhile. If you enjoy this book and any of my others, I would be grateful for a brief review on Amazon, Goodreads, your blog, and/or any of my social media sites.

ABOUT THE AUTHOR

Debbie De Louise is an award-winning author and a reference librarian at a public library on Long Island. She is a member of Sisters-in-Crime, International Thriller Writers, the Long Island Authors Group, and the Cat Writers' Association. Her novels include the five books and four stories of the Cobble Cove cozy mystery series, a comedy novella, *When Jack Trumps Ace*, a paranormal romance, *Cloudy Rainbow*, and the standalone mysteries; *Reason to Die*, *Sea Scope*, and *Memory Makers*. Debbie has also written a non-fiction cat book, *Pet Posts: The Cat Chats*, written from the points of view of four of her cats and has also published articles in online and print pet magazines including Catster.com. Her latest novel, *Time's Relative,* is a time-travel thriller.

Debbie's stories and poetry appear in the Red Penguin Collections, *What Lies Beyond, 'Tis the Season, Stand Out, Volumes I and II*. Her poems are also featured in the Nassau County *Voices In Verse* 2020 anthology and the 2020 *Bards Annual*. She lives on Long Island with her husband, daughter, and three cats.

Connect with Debbie on her website and social media sites:

Website/Blog/Newsletter Sign-Up: https://debbiedelouise.com

Meows And Purrs
ISBN: 978-4-86752-978-2
Mass Market

Published by
Next Chapter
1-60-20 Minami-Otsuka
170-0005 Toshima-Ku, Tokyo
+818035793528

3rd October 2021